In a Heartbeat

"The Last German-Estonian Immigrant"

von Kiparski

In a Heartbeat

"The Last German-Estonian Immigrant"

Christa Eckert Blum

Psalm 117

Christa Eckert-Blum

Pleasant Word
A Division of WINEPRESS PUBLISHING

Printed in the United States of America

Packaged by Pleasant Word, a division of WinePress Publishing, PO Box 428, Enumclaw, WA 98022. The views expressed or implied in this work do not necessarily reflect those of Pleasant Word, a division of WinePress Publishing. Ultimate design, content, and editorial accuracy of this work are the responsibilities of the author.

ISBN 1-4141-0252-6
Library of Congress Catalog Card Number: 2004095818

Dedication

This book is dedicated to
Ariana, Jennifer, Juliana, Janine,
Jordon and Jaimen.

Table of Contents

Introduction

Wake up, Mom! Wake up, Mom! my daughter Lynn shook me gently to arouse me from a deep sleep. I didn't want to wake up. I was feeling comfortable in aisle seat 14C on a flight full of vacationers bound for a warmer climate and sunny beaches. Only twenty minutes into the flight, Lynn insisted I wake up, trying to detect a pulse in my wrist. "Talk to me," she demanded. But instead of a reply, I promptly threw up the whole breakfast I had washed down with a kiwi-strawberry drink at the airport food court before departure.

My physician daughter Lynn promptly contacted the flight attendant and said her mother's situation was life-threatening. Dr. Lynn suggested that the pilot land at the next available airport. (He didn't want a corpse on his six-hour vacation flight.) Since no announcement came from the cockpit: "This is your captain speaking . . .," the tourists on board probably wondered why their non-stop flight was suddenly making an unscheduled landing. People craned their necks to see a woman hobble down the aisle delaying their long-awaited vacation by at least two hours.

I could have faded away in a heartbeat. Instead, I was rushed away in an ambulance with sirens blaring. Why me? Why did I have to miss a great vacation and end up in the hospital on Epiphany? My brother volunteered a plausible answer: "You know, our grandfather died on January 6." Well, thanks a lot for this bit of history. I never knew that, but I certainly experienced my own epiphany during my hospital stay and subsequent recovery in our home overlooking beautiful Scenic Park in Lakewood, Ohio.

Three weeks have passed since I had open-heart surgery on January 6, 2003. Morning sunshine floods through the bank of windows encircling our living room with a view of the snowy landscape outside. Mist is rising from the valley, giving the bare trees a foggy background, outlining the trunks and branches in an impressionistic way. A mighty oak tree, at least 250 years old, stands at the edge of the cliff at the middle of the gray picket fence that guards the steep drop to the Rocky River below. Centuries ago Chippewa Indians used this plateau as a lookout point to the bend of the river. Now this bend-in-the-river location in the stream is a favorite spot for fishermen angling for steelhead trout. The snow has melted on the evergreen bushes. They stand like round green sentinels along the cliff. No new snow has fallen. The American flag is at half-mast in our front yard because the space shuttle Columbia exploded upon entering the earth's atmosphere. All seven astronauts have perished in a heartbeat. No one knows as yet what happened. Bob woke up, came downstairs and announced he'll cook a solid breakfast for me. I need a good, morning meal. The surgeon ordered hearty meals for me to regain my strength after major surgery. During my recovery from open-heart surgery, I had many visitors, family and friends. Each time they come, I think, I must write down my story before I fade away in a heartbeat.

CHAPTER 1

Trip to Estonia

When a brown envelope came in the mail one day in the spring of 1999, my husband smiled knowingly and gave it to me to open. There in this large envelope was information with registration papers for a trip to Tallinn, Estonia, to visit and encourage the United Methodist churches in that Baltic region. "I thought you would like to see the place where you were born," Bob said with a grin. Never in my wildest dreams had I imagined that I would return to the place of my birth on a Volunteers-in-Mission (VIM) trip.

We signed up immediately for this trans-Atlantic journey scheduled for September of that same year. When we arrived in Tallinn and visited the Baltic Methodist churches, it was the singing of the Estonians that stirred memories of my childhood and of my Estonian mother. It was the passionate and fervent prayers of the Russian-speaking congregations that reminded me of my godly Russian grandmother. Everywhere we traveled, from Tallinn to Saarema, to Pärnu, to Riga my birthplace, I was reminded of where I came from, of what my parents had left behind when they fled with their young family from the advancing Soviet troops and finally landed in America, the land of dreams come true.

Dreams have come true for the Baltic States as well. Churches that were closed and empty for more than fifty years are now being renovated and rebuilt, an answer to the fervent prayers of Christians everywhere. "I remember when Oma and Opa prayed every night for the Word of God to be preached again in their homeland," my daughter Karin reminded me. Even though my parents never returned to their homeland in their lifetime, they remained faithful in their intercession for those denied religious freedom.

When our VIM team entered the 500-year-old church in Umurga, Latvia, where my Baltic-German ancestors had worshipped, I was in awe of God's infinite power, His majesty, His steadfastness. The clergymen in our group broke bread and shared the cup with the eight-member Friends-of-Estonia Team. It was an unforgettable communion experience for me.

Our journey continued on to Liepaja on the Baltic coast where we worshipped with a Latvian congregation. They greeted us with joyous song, accompanied by a pianist and cellist. After our team was introduced to the Latvians, we also sang, accompanied on the guitar by one of our team members. On this trip through the Baltic countryside, I felt we were being served. The hospitality of the congregations we visited was generous and genuine. The meals were typically Baltic, sardines and herring with sour cream served on slices of dark crusty bread and hot tea prepared in a Russian samovar.

It was the conversation around the table, understood in my limited Russian, that opened my eyes to the suffering these Christians had endured. Thousands of innocent victims had been deported to Siberian hard-labor camps. Many never returned. On the island of Saarema stands a memorial dedicated to those who died in Siberia. But here around the supper table were two women who had returned home, who had become grandmothers, and who lived their faith so that others could be free. Words failed me.

Later we met the Rev. Olav Parnamets, superintendent of the Estonian United Methodist Church. He was so excited about the construction of a new Baltic Mission Center in Tallinn. His face would not admit to the suffering he also experienced under Communism. His steadfast faith allowed him to see the beginning and completion of this new seminary and sanctuary. The young faces of the seminary students we met showed the confidence and assurance that God would bring to completion the task begun in Estonia.

Lutheran Church, built 1496, Umurga, Latvia

Saarema, Estonia, Memorial to Victims who died in World War II Siberian Labor Camps.

CHAPTER 2

My Estonian Relatives

I wondered as we arrived in Estonia that September day whether this trip was my very first journey to the land where my mother was born.

We were eight Americans traveling in a van in Estonia when suddenly we heard a familiar tune. It wasn't the radio, but our driver's cell phone ringing out: Happy birthday to you, happy birthday, etc. The driver answered the ring and said something in Estonian as he kept on driving along the bucolic country road overshadowed by white-stemmed birch trees so prominent in that Baltic region. My birthday was only two days away on this warm September day. The tune reminded me that Estonians don't celebrate birthdays the same way Americans do. I doubt that our Estonian chauffeur even knew that the cell phone ring was an American birthday song. Growing up with an Estonian mother and German father, I never heard that tune until I came to America as a young teen. When we celebrated birthdays, it was not with pink birthday candles. But my mother baked a raisin-filled *kringel,* which is shaped like a huge pretzel. Then my family gathered around the table, my mother cut slices of the delicious raisin bread, we sat down to eat, and maybe I even received a present.

I definitely felt a connection to the Estonian people. The language seemed familiar and the people reminded me of my mother as a young woman. I remember seeing a black and white photo in my mother's album. She and her sister Emmi were standing on a beach. In the foreground were six children, cousins in fact, sitting on a ferocious-looking crocodile, mounted on cement blocks on the beach. The three older children were my aunt Emmi's children, and between them sat my two brothers. I was the youngest child, sitting on the lap of my cousin Lea. It was the summer of 1936, and I was less than a year old. Now I realized that the beach was the stretch of land along the Baltic Sea where my aunt Emmi had lived. Her daughter Daimi still lives there. She married Freddi Korjus in 1953 in Tallinn, and they had two daughters, Anne and Helle. On September 18, 1999, Bob and I tried to contact Anne. In my diary I wrote that day:

> Nothing on the agenda today, except trying to find Daimi. After several phone calls, which a lady at Poska Villa (where we stayed overnight) made for me, I found out that Daimi's husband Freddi had died last year. Daimi is in Hapsaal with her older daughter. Her younger daughter Anne is here in Tallinn, working and staying at the apartment at Tamasaare.

Sunday afternoon, Bob and I took a taxi to the apartment complex where Anne lives. Along the way we bought a bouquet of flowers, as it is customary to bring a small gift. The taxi driver, who knew some English, was very helpful in finding the apartment building on the edge of town. It was a quiet, sunny day and we walked from the taxi to the eight-story, cinder-block buildings, which all looked alike. Finally finding the number 98–6, we bravely rang the doorbell. No answer, we continued ringing and knocking, causing some neighbors to peek out from behind the window curtains. But no one came to open the front door. So we put the flowers next to the row of mailboxes for Anne and left in the same taxi we had arrived in. I was sad that I did not meet any of my mother's relatives in Estonia.

But we did get to meet Lucia Kahars in Riga, my mother's niece, daughter of her brother Leo. His son, Viktor Kahar, like so many other young men during WWII had been drafted into the Deutsche Wehrmacht (German Army). After the war, he emigrated to Brazil. There is an extensive Kahar family clan living in Brazil. When we visited his sister, Lucia Kahars in Riga in 1999, she showed us a whole family album and gave us a number of family photos. She never married, but she was very active with the Latvian Girl Scouts, becoming a leader and mentor to the young girls. Lucy is also active in the church. Singing in the choir is one of her favorite activities. During the Communist era, there were no Methodist or Baptist churches in Latvia, but now there are ten or even more.

When we arrived in Riga, after checking into the Laine Hotel in the center of town, we took a taxi first to Vilandes iela to see the house I had lived in as a three-year-old. It was a beautiful renovated walk-up apartment, now with offices of the German Siemens company. I remember living in a large house, where we shared a living room with Tante Leni's family. A grand piano dominated the great room. Music was always an important part of our family. Tante Leni played the piano, Papa played the guitar, and Mama sang.

It was the singing that set the people free. Communism could not kill the song of faith and hope and love that was in the souls of the Latvian, Estonian and Russian peoples. After the fall of the Communist Regime, the Baltic States gained their independence in 1991. Bob and I took a walk down Brivibas iela, which means Freedom Street. During the Soviet era it was called Stalin iela, before that the Hitler iela, and in the Czarist time it was known as Alexander iela. Freedom has won the victory in this Baltic land.

Olav Parnaments, our host on the 1999 VIM trip, told about his experience under Communism. One day when his family went to Saarema for a speaking engagement and sightseeing, the Communists arrested him and locked him up. He got a telephone call and had to answer all kinds of questions and was not free to go where he wanted to on Saarema. Now our American VIM team, along with Olav, was taking the ferry to Saarema without incident. How times have changed. After arriving at the town Kuressare, we shopped at the open-air market where merchants displayed hand-carved souvenir spoons, plates, and toys. A row of hand-knit sweaters, gloves, and hats formed a backdrop for the display tables. Buckets full of fresh asters in autumn shades of Baltic blue, white, pink, and rose stood near the tables with an array of vegetables, potatoes, carrots, parsley, and beets bountifully arranged in baskets, crates, and containers.

After buying some souvenirs, we drove on to the cemetery where Martin Prikask, who founded the first Methodist Church in Estonia, is buried. It was very moving to see all these memorials to fallen soldiers, Germans, Russians and Estonians. Many of the German landed Gentry are buried there on Saarema. We visited the fortification on Saarema dating back to 1340 and mentioned in a chronicle of 1381. The castle is a museum now and open to the public. There we viewed an extensive photo exhibit of 1941–44 showing people escaping on boats from the advancing Soviet troops–destination, Sweden. Almost four hundred years earlier Johannes von Münchhausen sold the castle to the Danes who fortified it with a moat and bastions. In 1645 Sweden obtained the island Ösel or Saarema through a contract. Then in 1710 the castle was taken by Russian troops without resistance from the Swedish garrison who were suffering from the black plague. In 1836 the castle went to a knighted family who named the castle Ahrensburg, Burg des Adlers (eagle's castle), and the settlement around it was named Ahrensburg.

Haapsal Beach along the Gulf of Finland. Author's mother Lisa with her children and Estonian cousins with their mother, Tante Emmi.

Market Day on Saarema.

Youth Group and Papa with guitar on left.

CHAPTER 3

How We Escaped the Russians

The 1941–44 photo exhibit on Saarema Island showed me what our family was spared when my parents left Riga with the "grosse Umsiedlung" (evacuation) in 1939 and settled in Posen, which was then part of Germany. My father, an ethnic German, and all Germans living in the Baltic countries were called upon to return to Germany because of what was called the Ribbentrop Pact, an agreement made between Soviet Russia and Nazi Germany to relinquish the Baltic countries to Soviet rule.

My brother Kuno, then seven, cried because he was not allowed to take his favorite wooden rocking horse with him on the boat. Who would take possession of his horse with that fine leather saddle? I don't remember crying.

I have fond memories of living in Posen where I started to go to school.

I made friends with some of my classmates and visited their homes after school. We liked to put on little skits and invited our parents to our dramatic shows. We also liked to visit the Zoo with our friends. My father's sister Tante Leni, and her three children had moved to Gnesen from Riga. So we saw them in the summer when we spent the hot summer days at Talsee and stayed in a little cottage nearby. We collected pinecones, "schiskas," wore straw hats, and had a wonderful summertime.

When school started, we traveled back to Posen. I remember the warning sirens alarming us of air attacks and causing us to run downstairs into the basement until the bombing attacks were over. One Sunday after such an attack, we walked to the part of the city where my school friend lived. I remember her house was bombed. Ours remained standing.

My father was on the Russian front with the German "Luftwaffe" (air force) as a Russian language expert. We received word that we would have to leave Posen because the Soviet troops were advancing to the west. From what I remember, we went to the mobbed train station and somehow caught the last train out of Posen to I don't know where.

My older brother Kuno wrote about our escape ten years later for his college English class. In 1955, Kuno von Kiparski was a freshman at Western Reserve University in Cleveland, Ohio, when he wrote:

"How We Escaped the Russians."

> I remember many incidents of my childhood. One is most clearly imprinted in my memory: I will never forget Saturday, the 19th of January, 1945, the beginning of our long flight from the Russians. I went to school as usual the day before, never guessing the dreadful events which were going to happen in the week ahead. I came home, did my homework, and when we parted late that night, I promised my friends to go skiing with them the next day.
>
> Then on Saturday, our city paper proclaimed with huge headlines that all civilians had to leave the city within twenty-four hours for it had been declared a fortress and was supposed to be defended against the oncoming Russian tank division, already only some thirty miles away. This news shocked us all. We never suspected the Russians (Soviets)

to be that close to us because we trusted in our armed forces. My father was with the air force in Russia and could not help or advise us where to go. Our safety depended mostly on our speed. My mother was desperate; she did not know how to get us three children out of the town. Just then, a woman who knew my mother from church arrived on foot and out of breath from across town and urged my mother to go to the train station and leave Posen immediately. For fear of being captured by enemy troops, my mother took her advice.

After hours of frantic packing, we were ready to go to the station. I looked around our home as we left and cried for I knew I would never see it again. The few bundles and suitcases we had with us could never hold all the things and memories that were valuable and dear to us for we had to fill them with practical articles.

There were already thousands of people in or around the station, desperately trying to get on a train. We had to push very hard to get into the building. We made it, finally. We knew the stationmaster very well, and he helped us to get out to the tracks. There we waited all night for the train. It was very cold outside, and we were very close to freezing. It was heartbreaking to see the mothers cry for their children who got lost in the large crowd.

On Sunday morning, a train pulled into the station. I don't know what would have happened if a compartment door had not stopped right in front of us with an open window next to it. Seeing my mother struggling to get in with three small children, the person at the open window called out to hold up the children. He reached down, pulled my sister and other little ones up into the compartment, and we followed through the open door, hanging onto our mother's arms. Were it not for that helping hand, we probably would have been left behind with those thousands of distraught civilians on "Bahnsteig 4" (Track 4). I could see and feel their despair, as the train pulled away. It was the last train to leave Posen.

We did not have the slightest idea where we were heading, but one thing was certain–each minute on the train took us farther away from the dreadful enemy. Many times though, we were attacked by low-flying planes, and we hoped and prayed that the bullets would miss.

We were supposed to go through Dresden, but fate saved us again for the train stopped just outside the city. Late that night, all of Dresden was destroyed in one of the worst air raids in the history of the war. We could see the flames soar up into the dark sky, painting it fiery red. Soon a storm came up, and the river Elbe started to rise. Many people were drowned on the banks of the river where they fled to escape the intense heat. I remember one man standing dazed at the river looking at one shoe that he was holding in his hand.

We were five days on the train. Occasionally, the Red Cross was able to give us hot coffee and bread, or hot soup. Then one night, we stopped in a town. We had to leave the train and were directed into a large hall, which kind people had turned into a dormitory. Soon we would be lodged in private homes, they told us. I fell asleep the minute I lay down. When I opened my eyes late next morning, I hardly could believe what I saw. Almost right in front of the window rose the high peaks of the Alps. I had always wanted to see the Alps, but I never dreamed it would be in this fashion.

We were in Berchtesgaden (Bavaria), I learned later. There we anxiously awaited the arrival of the enemy forces who finally moved into the city after the armistice was signed. They were Americans!

Posen. Christa at the Zoo with Mama Lisa and Tante Lydia and friends.

Posen. von Kiparski family with Onkel Hartmann.

Christa in Talsee, Summer Resort, with brothers and cousin Boris.

CHAPTER 4

End of War

The years at the end of the war, May of 1945 to 1946, were spent in Bavaria where we lived on a secluded farm called Stöckeln. My two brothers had to walk four kilometers to the village school. This became difficult because of the low-flying enemy airplanes looking for people or things to attack. The local school kids called my brothers "Preußi Teifi" (Prussian Devils) because we were Protestants and refugees from the East. There was enough name-calling to drive my brothers away from school and they stopped going to the village.

Life on Stöckeln in the countryside, however, was really good for us. The owner of the farm and his family took us in as their own. We did not starve like thousands of people during the end-of-the-war days. Many times we ate at the farmer's table. The daily meal was "Dampfnudeln" or "Knödel," a type of Bavarian specialty of dumplings and round noodles served with a soup.

I learned where chicken soup came from and watched the farmer's wife milk the cows. The horse stable was kept clean with hay from the barn where I also liked to go and look for the eggs that the chicken had laid somewhere in the loft. It was an adventure finding the eggs.

I also remember the cold, snowy winter of 1946. On Christmas Eve, we hiked through the deep snow to go to the nearby village to attend Midnight Mass. I had never before been inside a Catholic church. As we entered this house of God, I remember how cold and dim it was inside this tall edifice. A wintry glow shone through the window arches. The priest at the altar was swinging a round vessel like a pendulum. "Das ist Weihrauch," my mother whispered to me. The scent of incense filled the air. It was a strangely new and at the same time fascinating worship experience. I was glad to be in a safe sanctuary, not far from Oberndorf, where on another Christmas more than a hundred years ago Franz Gruber wrote the now famous hymn, "Stille Nacht, Heilige Nacht."

CHAPTER 5

Who Were the Prussians?

Prussian Devils we were not. However, my family comes from Kiparen, a village in East Prussia. Under King Sigismund, the family was ennobled and the name became Kiparski or "of Kiparen." In the early eighteenth century, one member of the Kiparen family immigrated to Livland and settled in Cesis or "Wenden" in German. This is my lineage. For 200 years my family was part of the history of this area called Livland. In 1919 it became part of the State of Latvia and Estonia.

Who were the Prussians? History records that in 1235 the Teutonic Knights or German Knights were commissioned by King Ottokar of

Bohemia to help Christianize the pagan Prussian tribes (heidnischen wilden Pruzzen) and also the Lithuanian tribes. The knights founded the city of Thorn (where Copernicus was born in 1473) and built a fortress called Malbork or Marienburg at the river Nogat in Poland. It is the largest fortification built entirely of red bricks around a courtyard with a well at the center. Malbork castle is still in existence. Bob and I visited there in 1998. More than a thousand people lived in that fortification, a city that sustained itself.

The daily tasks started with prayer in the Chapel of St. Mary. The thirty-foot statue of Mary was destroyed during WWII and never rebuilt. Besides three chapels, it had a hospital, a dungeon and a jail, a kitchen, several dining halls, and a number of grand halls and living quarters. The outhouse was at the top floor and its door was embellished with gruesome gargoyles, a warning to keep the visit short.

The Teutonic Knights became quite powerful and settled in the land that came to be known as East Prussia (Ostpreussen). The coat of arms of the Teutonic Knights was the Christian cross on the white flag (see picture) and their motto was "In Treuen Fest," which means to be faithful and true in the service to others: treu sein und dienen. By the way, the motto of the British Monarchy is: Ich dien! from the German: I serve.

In 1255 the Teutonic Knights founded the city of Königsberg, now known as Kaliningrad and part of Russia. Bordering East Prussia is Lithuania and Poland. The Knights were expanding and settling in the Baltic region. Lithuania became Christian and formed an alliance with Poland through the marriage of the Polish Princess Jadwiga to the Lithuanian Count Jagiello who became King of Lithuania in the fifteenth century. With the help of the Polish army and the Lithuanian troops, the Teutonic Knights were defeated at the "Battle of Tannenberg" in 1410. The Knights retreated to Marienburg under Count Conrad von Erlichhausen. His statue is standing to this day at the castle Malbrok/Marienburg. The Polish king defeated the knights in 1457. Then the Teutonic Knights made Königsberg their residence.

In later centuries, Königsberg became known for its famous residents, such as philosopher Immanuel Kant, storyteller E.T.A. Hoffmann, artist Kaethe Kollwitz, and many others, including Albrecht von Brandenburg who founded the University of Königsberg in 1544.

Descendants of the Teutonic Knights became known as the Landed Gentry of Prussia, Livland and Kurland. Livland is the land, which is now

Latvia and Estonia where my ancestors settled. Wissust near Tartu, Ronneburg near Raunao, and Roperbeck near Umurga were three of the baronial estates, where the von Kiparski family lived and where the 500-year-old Lutheran church is still standing. The manor houses have been destroyed, only the massive stone church at Umurga remains with records containing the names of the von Kiparski family who worshipped there.

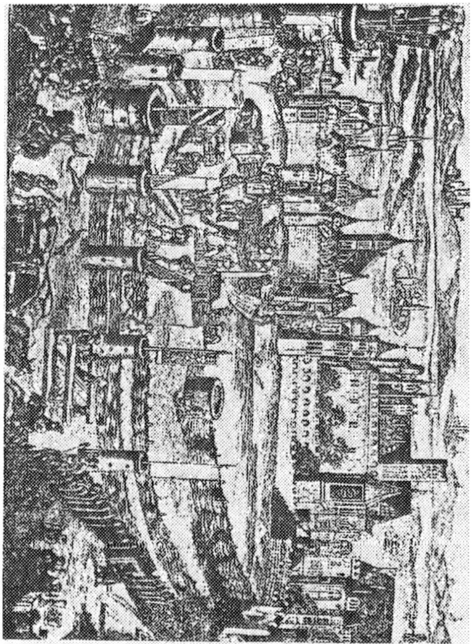

Malbork/Marienburg Castle. In Treuen Fest, shield

Count Conrad von Erlichhausen

Christa and Robert Blum with "Teutonic Knight."

CHAPTER 6

My Father's Family

My grandmother's name was not part of the church records in Umurga. She was born in 1886 of Russian parents, and her name was Marie Savelyeva. Like so many young women around the turn of the century, she sought work in the big city of Riga.

Woldemar von Kiparski was a prominent citizen of Riga. He owned a stable of horses and baronial estates Roperbeck and Maikendorf. He was thirty-three years old, a lawyer and a bachelor and needed help running his household. His four brothers and five sisters were pursuing their own academic and artistic careers and couldn't help him look for a housemaid. One of Woldemar's friends suggested that pretty eighteen-year-old Marie Savelyeva could help out running his Riga residence. Marie learned quickly how to please, from cooking Russian borscht to making beds. So it was no surprise when in 1904 Eugen, who became my father, was born to Marie and Woldemar. Three more children, Leni, Woldemar, and Axel, were born to Marie and Woldemar. But my grandfather never found time to marry Marie.

My father Eugen was always called Jhenya, which is the Russian diminutive of Eugen. His mother Marie spoke only Russian with him. Jhenya spoke German with his father and Latvian with his Latvian friends. He studied to become a teacher and taught at the orphanage in Riga. He was a deeply religious man. He married my mother, Elisabeth Kahar, an Estonian who, like Marie, had come to Riga to look for work. He played the guitar at the Latvian Baptist Church, and my mother Lisa sang along in her lovely soprano voice. When their first child Kuno was born in 1932, my father demanded that Grandpapa Woldemar von Kiparski make an honest woman of his housekeeper/mistress and marry her. And so it was that Marie Savelyeva became Marie von Kiparski. Grandfather experienced his own epiphany in 1935 when he died on that day, January 6, leaving behind his 49-year-old widow Marie.

I never knew my grandfather because I grew up only knowing my Russian grandmother whom I called Oma. I thought it was perfectly normal to have only one grandmother. She spoke Russian with me and sang and prayed with me. She had a secret rosary which she called a "Rosenkranz." I never saw it and could not figure out where and why she kept her wreath of roses in order to pray. The German word *Rosenkranz* literally means "wreath of roses."

I also never knew my grandparents on my mother's side, Mart Kahar and Marie Jaama. Both were born in 1874 in Tartu, Estonia, and died there in the 1920s. Grandmother Marie died in 1960 at a time when I was already living in America.

Marriage of Eugen von Kiparski and Elisabeth Kahar (center).
Marie Savelyeva and Woldemar von Kiparski (on right).
Tante Leni (behind Elisabeth).

Elisabeth and Eugen von Kiparski with firstborn child Kuno, Riga.

Elisabeth and Eugen in hammock with Christa,
Hans and Kuno, Riga.

Oma and Christa

CHAPTER 7

Living in America

So how did I get to America? At the end of WWII in 1945, my mother, my two brothers and I had escaped to Bavaria. The war had ended, leaving thousands of people without a place to live. These were called displaced persons or refugees. The Allied Forces divided conquered Europe into four zones, the American Sector, the British Sector, the French Sector, and the Soviet Sector. They tried to relocate these refugees who had lost house and home into one of those sectors.

It was a very difficult and tragic time for those who escaped from the advancing Soviet armies and now had no place to go. It is the deathly holocaust story of the Donauschwaben, the Banater, of displaced ethnic Germans. Thousands of refugees escaped on foot, by horse and wagon, on trains with no destination. Tens of thousands were slaughtered and executed. Others escaped on ships in the Baltic Sea. One of these refugee ships, *The Wilhelm Gustloff*, was torpedoed by a Russian submarine and 10,000 men, women, and children lost their lives in the icy waters of the Baltic Sea on January 30, 1945. These were the forgotten refugees of the Second World War, and for years nothing was written about these innocent victims.

We were fortunate to have friends that we knew from Riga in the city of Marburg, located in the Grimm's fairy-tale land of Hessen. My parents had made an agreement that if we get separated during the war, we would contact Lisbeth Kratin in Marburg. My father was a prisoner of war. He was fluent in Russian, and his Soviet commander did not want to let him go because he served as an able interpreter. However his Russian commander was transferred to the Japanese front, and thus my father was released to go to Marburg where he contacted Lisbeth Kratin and found out where the rest of the family was.

We came to the village of Todenhausen near Marburg where my father received a teaching position. We lived in this schoolhouse for three years. Papa was the teacher in the one-room school for the local children. I enrolled in that village school for maybe a year, and then my older brother and I attended the prep school (Gymnasium) in Marburg. We had to take the train every day to the city and were know as *Fahrschüler*, which means 'commuters'.

Upon arrival at Marburg's main train station, Hauptbahnhof, I had a twenty-minute walk to the Elisabethschule near the Phillips University.

Every day on my way to school, I passed the Sankt Elisabeth Kirche, a magnificent Gothic cathedral named for Princess Elisabeth of Hungary. At age twelve I did not give much thought to any saints, let alone St. Elisabeth. It was in 1998 that I had the opportunity to visit the Wartburg Castle in Thuringia, Germany, where Princess Elisabeth had lived in the thirteenth century as a young bride. She became the mother of four children and was widowed at age twenty-four when her husband died in the crusades to the Holy Land. Princess Elisabeth had to leave the Wartburg Castle after she was widowed. She ministered to the poor and the sick and founded a hospital for them in Marburg. She was a true saint. I have known many women called Elisabeth, my late mother among them, who were worthy of sainthood.

One of my school friends in Marburg was Reinhild Trautz, daughter of a well-to-do merchant who owned a dry-goods store. The family lived above the commercial company in a spacious apartment. Sometimes my train to Marburg arrived early, too early to go directly to the school building. So after first walking past the Sankt Elisabeth Kirche, the Botanical Gardens, the Phillips University and my school, I'd turn left and down the Margareten street to my friend Reinhild's residence. Occasionally I'd join the Trautz's for breakfast. Frau Trautz always read a Bible passage at the breakfast table before we ate. Reinhild had an older brother Karl and an older sister Magdalena who later married and moved to Sweden.

Reinhild and I became good friends, and we attended the Baptist Church together located at Roten Graben. One Sunday morning worship we both went to the altar when after the sermon the minister gave an invitation to come forward to accept Jesus as our Saviour. I cried and was so convicted of my sins. Later Reinhild and I were baptized by immersion by our minister Reverend Wessel. We started a little Bible Study, and we encouraged each other in our Christian faith. I visited Reinhild in 1982 when I flew to Germany because my brother Hans had died suddenly, leaving his wife and three children, Hans-Hagen, Kuno-Kornelius and Christiane. By then Reinhild was also married and had two sons. That was the last time I saw my school friend. Five years later Reinhild died of breast cancer.

Another school friend I had was Renate von Baumbach who lived in nearby Amönau. Later her family moved to Bad Homburg where I visited her in their elegant family residence. Her sister Angela became a flight attendant and married an American, moving to America with him. He died and Angela now lives on the West Coast. Her sister Renate, my classmate, died of a brain tumor in 1991, leaving a husband and four children.

It was also in Marburg that I started to visit the America House which had programs about America. We learned Negro spirituals like, "Go down Moses" and "It's Me, It's Me, O Lord, Standing in the Need of Prayer."

I always wondered what "It's me" meant. I thought, it was one word, "ITSME," and couldn't find it in the dictionary. Much later I found out that it was a contraction of "it is me" and that—"It is I"—is the correct expression. But with correct grammar the phrase would never have become a popular Spiritual. I still like to sing, "It's me, It's me, O Lord, Standing in the Need of Prayer."

I also learned to sing "My Old Kentucky Home" by Stephen Foster at the America House. When I finally visited Kentucky for the first time in 2002, I learned that Foster was born in Pittsburgh, Pennsylvania. I thought that this Kentucky home was some kind of log cabin, but I was surprised to see the stately mansion of Judge Rowan, a relative of Foster, who lived in Bardstown. It was there that Foster wrote this song, which is now Kentucky's state anthem. So I learned many cultural aspects about America when I was living in Germany.

Christa's School Class on field trip to Frankfurt/ Main

CHAPTER 8

Displaced Persons Camp

When my parents decided to immigrate to the USA in 1951, it was with much anticipation that I looked forward to this move. There were many preparations before we could immigrate to America. We stayed in a displaced persons camp in Hanau (photo) until we, together with many other emigrants, boarded the SS *General Eltinge* on a cold December morning in Bremerhaven.

I was fifteen years old and had lived in Todenhausen and later in Kirchhain for about five years. Leaving behind many school friends, I was envied for this adventure that lay ahead. In my German diary, I recorded some of the events leading up to our departure from Bremerhaven:

> On November 6, 1951 we arrived in Hanau where we stayed at a large housing complex with many other emigrants. My parents and my two brothers and I were assigned two rooms. We shared bathroom facilities with another family of five. But we could only bathe on Tuesdays and Fridays.
>
> The food is good, I wrote in my diary. For lunch we always eat meat and potatoes and sandwiches in the evening along with coffee to drink, very seldom tea. During the ten days we stayed at Hanau, we had our physical exams, including blood and urine samples, x-rays and small pox vaccinations for me. We were classified into Group B. In the afternoon there was an advanced reading group, which I attended. Sometimes a film about America was shown.
>
> On our tenth day in Hanau, the American Consul interrogated us. We were photographed and fingerprinted and had to sign our names. We had to swear before the Consul that all our answers on the questionnaire were correct. He also asked us if we ever belonged to the Communist Party or were ever con-

victed of a crime. He didn't ask me anything, I think, because I was too young.

We also had to go to the Immigration Inspector who was hard of hearing, spoke only English and was in a bad mood. He asked the meaning of the abbreviated "v. Kiparski" and on another form there was written "von Kiparski." What was the meaning of this, he demanded. The secretary patiently interpreted that Mr. Kiparski always writes "v. Kiparski" but was asked to write out the complete name thus: von Kiparski. The Inspector wanted to know what *Frauenwerk* and *Volksgemeinschaft* meant. The secretary, who was very nice, said: "Those are welfare organizations." She was annoyed with the inspector because he found fault with everything. At one point she stuck out her tongue at him, behind his back, of course. She was helpful and saw to it that we got through all the red tape as quickly as possible. Mama was exhausted at the end of that interview. It was really sad to hear, when we returned to Hanau for our final departure, that this young secretary had drowned by driving her car into the Kinzig River in Hanau.

For the next two weeks, we packed our things. We said farewell to our friends in Marburg,

Kirchhain, Todenhausen and Hassenhausen. Everyone was sad that we were leaving for America. Mama had no more tears left because she had cried so much. For the final time we boarded a train from our home to Hanau with all our belongings. We were on our way to Bremerhaven, where on December 17th we boarded the SS *General Eltinge.*

Hanau, Germany, U.S. Displaced Persons Camp.
Christa, her mother, Hans, and Father Eugen
(left to right).

CHAPTER 9

Aboard Ship

Wir sind auf dem Schiff (we are on the ship), I wrote in my German diary:

> We walked around the deck. We are assigned sleeping quarters, bunk beds stacked three to four cots high. There are cold showers and toilet stalls without doors. Men and women were separated. I stayed with Mama, and my brothers stayed with Papa. Because of the dense fog, the ship left some time during the night, "um Mitternacht," I recorded in my diary. When I woke up the next day, we were already on the high seas. It was six o'clock in the morning, and we heard the call to rise

and come for breakfast. We had hard-boiled eggs, toast, fruit jello and coffee. It tasted pretty good until I felt a queasiness in my stomach and raced up on deck to breathe in the fresh air, which helped to stabilize me. I climbed down to our cabin, took a Dramamin tablet, a sip of cognac and felt much better. In the afternoon we heard the first alarm bell, which meant to put on our life vests. When the second alarm sounded we had to be on deck. It was very stormy outside, and we were allowed to go back to our cabins. Five minutes later the alarm sounded again, and this time we had to put on our life vests again. Turns out some people had ignored the signal and stayed in their cabins. This time the ship's crew made sure everyone was on deck with life vests on–Just a safety drill.

In the evening, everyone received one dollar and fifty cents. But we had to use up the money aboard ship because it was a coupon. In the PX store we could buy all kinds of goodies. I bought hazelnuts and a chocolate bar. There was a community room aboard ship where one could sit and read or talk to other passengers or just listen to the sound of many languages, Estonian, Latvian, Russian, Italian, Czech, Polish, and only seldom

German. There were Jewish people on the ship, too. They kept to themselves at their own table in the dining hall. By the way, one had to stand up when eating there, no chairs, for a quick exit in case of seasickness.

One day a storm was predicted, and all passengers had to go below deck. The ship was moving through choppy waters, making it difficult to walk down below. Everything was swaying back and forth. The first two days aboard ship I was seasick, but I had grown sea legs. Only in the morning I was weak because I had not eaten breakfast yet. Mama went on deck every morning, so she wouldn't get sick from the swaying down below. We had to clean our cabin every morning. After ten o'clock, the inspector came and flashed a pocket light into every corner to check if everything was spotless.

The clocks have been set back four times already and still will be set back two more times. We are near Newfoundland, that's why it is so stormy outside. The captain promised his crew they'd be in New York for Christmas. Christmas Eve came and went without any mention of it. It was movie night again, and I didn't go. Instead I went down to our cabin where others had gathered and we sang "Stille Nacht, Heilige Nacht" and thought about home "zu Hause" wherever that might be.

On Christmas Day we had a worship service and in the afternoon St. Nicholas came to bring presents to the children up to age twelve. In the evening, we had a tasty turkey dinner and another movie night, which I missed again purposely. Later we heard singing up above, but I was too sleepy to go and sing.

Christmas is past and there is speculation as to when we will arrive in New York. Some predict we'll be there in three to four days. But the first officer on ship said that we will not be allowed into New York Harbor until the ship is in tip-top shape from top to bottom. After Christmas the sailors scrubbed the deck. In the afternoon all passengers had to be examined by the ship's doctor. In preparation for that, everyone washed and sponged clean, brushed teeth, changed underwear. I was quite nervous about seeing the doctor. There was a long line outside the doctor's office. Finally it was my turn. The doctor had a flashlight in one hand and a tongue depressor in the other. He said: "Open mouth," shines the flashlight down my throat, "Close mouth.

Pull up sweater," flashlight shines on my underwear. "Pull down sweater." Examination completed in less than five minutes.

New York, here we come!

Christa and Kuno aboard S.S. Eltinge.
"Wir sind auf dem Schiff."

CHAPTER 10

Arrival in America

"Schmecket und sehet wie freundlich der Herr ist."

From the 34th Psalm of David—"O taste and see that the Lord is good." (KJV)

This promise has followed me throughout my life in Europe and now in America. Arriving in America on December 29, 1951, remains forever in my memory. After a two-week voyage crossing the Atlantic Ocean, we were finally approaching the eastern coast of USA. All passengers were called through the loudspeaker: *Now hear this, now hear this: Dress warmly! Report to top-side to view the skyline.* There in the distance I saw lights in the darkness, like a sparkling necklace on black velvet. It was New York City at night. Closer and closer we approached the shore, and we could see more lights, skyscrapers, cars, houses, buildings, then colorful lights, not just white lights. The multi-colored lights were Christmas ornaments, we were told, still shining at the end of December. While we were waiting to disembark, reporters were allowed to come aboard and interview the newly arrived immigrants.

One "immigrant interview" took place decades later when my grandson Jaimen Shinn interviewed me for his class assignment. Here is what he wrote (October 8, 1994):

"Immigrant Interview"

> I interviewed my grandma. She came from Riga in Latvia.
>
> She came to America in two weeks on a boat coming from Europe cross the Atlantic Ocean. When she came into the New York Harbor everyone on the ship got excited and when she saw Brooklyn Bridge she said it looked like beads on a necklace.
>
> When she first put her foot on the land she felt excited because it was a new country and

she could not wait to meet her new American family. She also felt welcomed because she had many friends to greet her.

There were about 1800 men, women and children on board the "Steamship Eltinge." It left from Port Bremerhaven in West Germany. They all survived the long trip. When she arrived in NYC the Christmas lights were still up for the winter.

The weather for her wasn't very nice. It was chilly and very icy. The waves were choppy. But despite the bad weather, it was a safe trip. She was 15 years old back then in 1951. When the sea was stormy, my grandma got seasick and threw up. Yuk, gross! When she was on the ship she ate, slept and talked with the people on the ship and wrote in her diary. I would have been pretty scared!

The New Year 1952 brought an end to mass immigration to the United States. Our family had been one family of 12,554 persons who had qualified under the Displaced Persons Program for entry to the United States. Our drawn-out experience in the Hanau Immigration Camp had not been in vain. An article in *The New York Times*, January 2, 1952, is headlined:

Estonian Family Is Last Under US Refugee Act

Frankfurt, Germany, Jan. 1, 1952—A family from Soviet-ruled Estonia today became the last of 12,554 persons to qualify for entry to the United States under the three-year American displaced persons program.

Heino Heinla, 27, his 24-year-old wife Lia, and their daughters, Kaja, 2, and Uku, 3 months, were the last to receive displaced persons visas before the stroke of midnight. The new year brought an end to the mass immigration.

Some 129,000 persons remain in Germany's displaced persons camps—men and women who could not qualify for entry to the United States—or for whom no visas were available.
Displaced Persons Commissioner Henry Rosenfield said that every last visa authorized by Congress was used along with 11,000 extras obtained by 'begging, borrowing and stealing' from unfilled national quotas.

Even for some of our relatives who had thought about coming to America it was too late now. They stayed in Germany and carved out a living for themselves with the help of the Marshall Plan, which provided food and care packages to displaced persons.

Our final destination after we arrived in New York was Cleveland, Ohio. But first we were greeted by the Salvation Army and our friend, Sister Tarasenco. We were so glad to be on solid ground. But where was our baggage? While we were waiting for our meager belongings, we were richly fed, and we chatted with our Russian Sister Tarasenco. Later in the afternoon, a taxi took us the Lackawanna Railroad. In my diary I wrote in German:

> We arrived at the train station at 4 pm. Our train for Cleveland was scheduled for an 8 pm departure. We were hungry and tired, and I started to cry. Papa took me outside and showed me the brightly lit Christmas lights on trees and houses. I cried even more. Finally we boarded the train at 7:30. The compartments had upholstered seats and big windows. I couldn't sleep. I woke up just about every hour. We arrived in Buffalo around six o'clock in the morning. Here our seats were turned around because we were going in the direction toward Cleveland. A porter came into our compartment and invited us for breakfast in the dining car. At 9:30 am

we arrived in Cleveland. We were greeted by Reverend Valine the minister from the Bethel Baptist Church, which had sponsored our trip to America. Also the Latvian Pastor Barbins was there and Mr. Gunnerfeldt from Bethel Baptist. It was Sunday morning, and we were expected at the 11 o'clock worship service at Bethel Baptist. In two cars, they drove us to our destination, just in time to be introduced to the congregation.

I have no recollection or record of how I felt that Sunday morning. But this Swedish-American congregation was very generous and gracious. As sponsors of our family they made sure that we moved into a house, that my father had work at Nela Park, and that we all were provided for with clothing and food. My brothers and I soon became friends with the youth of the church. They invited us to all their meetings, their homes, outings to Lake Erie, and picnics in the park. I enrolled in the local high school.

CHAPTER 11

Americanized Immigrant

On April 17, 1953, *Collinwood Spotlight*, the student newspaper, published the following article about this high school student:

> Christa, Americanized Now, Tells of School in Germany
>
> How would you like to take fifteen subjects and go to school six days a week? Christa von Kiparski, 12B3 used to do that in Germany before she came to the United States. She has been here since January 1952.
>
> Christa, a friendly, blue-eyed blonde, was born in Latvia. Her family moved several

times while they lived in Europe. Marburg, Germany, was their home before crossing the ocean.

In Germany, the boys and girls go to separate schools. There was a high school for those who wanted to be engineers, one for commercial pupils, and one which prepared students for college. Christa took a train to school, as did many of the pupils. She attended the academic school.

An interesting feature of their schools was that the teachers changed classes when the bell rang, and the pupils stayed in the same room all day. During lunch period, everybody took his or her packed lunches into the yard to eat, unless it was very cold. When a person graduates from high school in Germany, he has already had, besides high school, the equivalent of two years of college.

Christa speaks English very well since she studied it in Europe for five years. She also took German, Latin, biology, geography, chemistry, physics, and music. Here at Collinwood she is majoring in languages and is planning to go to college and become a lab technician.

A member of the senior orchestra, Christa has been playing cello for a year. She played a wooden flute in Germany, but this instrument isn't used in the United States.

Perhaps we don't appreciate our good fortune, not having been without. Christa was impressed by all the luxuries we have that she didn't have.

She has many funny experiences here such as forgetting to get a tardy slip one day she was late and having to chase all over the building looking for a teacher she didn't even know. But she has made many friends and has become a real American.

I learned to drive a car at Collinwood High School. Another "funny" experience I had in high school was when I received a history textbook.

On the inside cover there was a notice pasted that read: Condition when lent________. The teacher looked at me and then at the book and said, "Write on the line 'poor.'" Well, I did, but inside my heart was pounding, and I was furious. I was not poor, I thought, and even the rich students get books from the school. So later I erased "poor" and left the line blank. I liked

English and music very much, and I don't know why I said I wanted to become a lab technician. When I received a scholarship to Flora Stone Mather College of Western Reserve University, I soon found out that dissecting frogs in the lab was my least favorite activity. I enjoyed French and English and did very well with foreign languages. I admired my French professor, how elegant she looked when she entered the classroom, dressed up and in high heels. Most of the time, she would sit on the edge of the desk and lecture in French. I thought that's what I would like to do when I finish school: teach foreign languages at a college. It would take almost thirty years, marriage, children, and subsequent widowhood before that dream would become a reality.

New U.S. Citizens, the von Kiparski family in Cleveland, Ohio,

Collinwood High School Senior Prom. Christa, front left.

Christa, Collinwood High School graduate.

CHAPTER 12

College Days

When I was a waitress during my college days, I was called a Stouffer girl.

The word waitress was never used by Stouffer's Restaurant. I worked part-time and on weekends. When I arrived at Stouffer's on Playhouse Square, I usually went in the back entrance and upstairs to the locker room. Rows of metal lockers lined the wall like in high school and each Stouffer girl had a lock to secure her street clothes, shoes and belongings in the clanky metal locker. All Stouffer girls had to wear starched café-au-lait colored uniforms with a full slip underneath and a detachable white collar safety-pinned to the dress neckline. To complete the outfit, we tied a little snow-white cocktail apron around our waist with a big bow in the back. The bow had to be just the right size or the hostess would send us back to the changing room. Of course we wore stockings secured by a garter belt. Our shoes also had to be a spotless white. We had a morning line-up where all waitresses working lunch had to show up and pass muster. The dining-room hostess who assigned tables to us made sure that we also wore hairnets and no jewelry of any kind. Then we met in the kitchen to familiarize ourselves with the day's menu. We could ask the chef any questions about the food items.

This was my first job I held as a college student. Not only that, but as a recent immigrant to America, I learned for the first time in my life about such entrees as Welsh Rarebit, Chipped Beef over Toast, and Chicken à la King with mashed potatoes and peas and carrots. A la King meant that the chicken was served over a biscuit. The favorite entrees among lawyers eating lunch at Stouffer's were Swiss Steak or Calf's Liver smothered with onions and bacon strips on top. I also memorized how to set a table correctly with the fork to the left of the placemat and the knife and spoon on the right. The favorite dessert choice was Stouffer's apple pie with a piece of cheese, if not cheese, then apple pie à la mode and a hot cup of coffee. Guests really liked that dessert. Personally I liked the lemon meringue pie, something I had never eaten before in Germany. Another dessert that the ladies asked for was tapioca pudding topped with a red maraschino cherry. I received good tips, especially from the lawyers who came regularly to Stouffer's.

Some of the girls were only cocktail waitresses. They wore black uniforms with a white collar and apron. They looked so elegant and were older than the part-time college girls. We looked up to them and had to ask them to serve the drinks to our lunch guests. Men usually asked for a Manhattan or a Martini and ladies for a Pink Lady. I had never had one of those drinks in my life. Years later when I was traveling alone and waiting in the airport lounge for my flight, I was brave enough to order a Pink Lady. Immediately a gentleman joined me and started a conversation with me. I was amused by the attention. I had no intention of picking up a traveling companion. I was only curious to finally find out what a Pink Lady tasted like.

There are no more Stouffer's Restaurants but Stouffer's still prepares delicious frozen meals that can be found in most upscale grocery stores.

Christa, college graduate, Western Reserve University.

Proud parents look on as Christa chats with Dr. Bartelmez (left to right).

CHAPTER 13

Widowhood

In 1960 I married Dr. Richard Eckert, a young family physician. We reared three children, Karin, Lynn and Thomas. We were active in church. When Richard and I took our first trip to Haiti to report on the Haitian Mission our church supported, Richard ended up staying there for a week to fill in for Dr. Bill Hodges.

Richard loved to travel to the Caribbean with me. We learned to scuba together, and he made underwater movies of our diving adventures. He also helped at Hôpital le Bon Samaritain in Haiti and brought back a filmed report. He rode the countryside of Haiti on horseback, camera in hand. When people met him on the road, they greeted him with: "Bon jour, mon Père," thinking he was the local priest. During his visit to Haiti, he met and shook and hands with Dictator "Papa Doc" Duvalier, which was caught on camera. Richard carried that snapshot in his wallet as a passport for future visits. He planned to spend retirement helping out at mission hospitals in the Caribbean and scuba diving in his free time. It was not to be. Richard died of a massive heart attack on April 12, 1985, shortly after Easter and just after having returned from a trip to the Caribbean.

Dr. Richard Eckert

I was very angry that he had died so suddenly without leaving me any clue what to do. A week after the funeral my children had returned to college, and I was alone in the house. I looked out the window at the tall, green grass and decided it needed to be mowed. So I went into the garage, pulled out the lawn mower, filled the tank with gasoline and pulled on the cord to start the engine . . . grrr, grrr, grrrrr it grumbled, but the motor would not start. I tried again, but no luck. I was frustrated and angry, I ran into the house, slammed the door and cried: "What good is all my church work, if I can't even start the lawn mower." It was 10 o'clock in the morning and there were no neighbors around to help me. I cried and sobbed and pounded at the wall. All at once the doorbell rang. I wondered who would come so early in the morning. I wiped my face and went to open the door. There was Janice, my church friend, who lived a few streets away from me. "I was just on my way to do some errands and wondered if you needed any help," she said cheerfully. Did I need help?

"Do you know how to start a lawn mower," I asked. "Oh, sure, I do that all the time at my place," and she went to the lawn mower still sitting in the driveway, gave it one pull of the starter cord, and the engine purred very nicely and kept on humming. I was stunned. "Thank you, Janice." She hugged me and hopped in her car and off she went, probably on another visit to help someone. Then I knew the Lord really cared about me, even in the little things.

People invited me to their homes for Sunday dinner after I was widowed. They met me for lunch, or they came to my home and shared a meal. After a year or so, the invitations dwindled. I had always loved to entertain when my husband was living, but I wondered how I could do it without him. I looked for occasions to invite people to my home. I learned a lot from this experience and wanted to share it with anyone who loves to entertain but doesn't have the courage to do it alone. I was a little scared, so I began by inviting three widows. I thought it would be non-threatening and easy. That was a mistake. It was a sad pity party. I vowed never to do it again, and I haven't.

I realized I needed people of all ages and backgrounds when entertaining. I invited the new choir director and his family for Sunday dinner. He and his wife were happy to accept my invitation. Their three little children filled the house with laughter. We sang, we talked, we played, and we ate. Never did a Sunday afternoon pass so quickly.

Another opportunity for opening my home arose when I had a baby shower for a young woman whose family refused to acknowledge the young man with whom she had eloped. No one was giving her a baby shower. I ached for her. I sent out a dozen invitations. We had the most wonderful surprise party for this young woman and her husband. They have a second baby now, and her family has embraced the two grandchildren. But it was tough going at first when she needed love and acceptance.

Entertaining visiting missionaries is always a special blessing. I had an open house for a missionary couple one Sunday after the evening service. That was quite a daring move; I had no idea how many people would come, so I sent out a dozen written invitations, just in case. A dozen people came, but not the twelve I had invited. The Lord knew just whom to send to my home—those who were truly interested in meeting the missionaries and not the ones I thought would come. Among the guests was a young woman who would spend the following summer in Cameroon.

Singing, too, has always been part of my life. I invited the ladies' ensemble in which I sang for a rehearsal party before the Christmas holidays. That was a hectic time for ensemble members and their families. It was somewhat painful for me, because my own family was so far away, and I sensed the pain of loss even more during the holidays. But concentrating on the music truly prepared my heart for the Advent season.

When a young singer came to town to perform in our local opera company, I had lunch with her. Then I realized that she did not know any people in this town except the professional singers who were also hired to sing in the opera. I called a few of my music and art lover friends and invited them to meet our featured soprano before opening night. We had a midweek buffet party for her. We ate and talked and sang so loud that the neighbors asked me the next day if anyone was getting married (meaning me). No, not yet, I said. I continued to offer hospitality "without grumbling" as written in the Scriptures. That was (and still is) the key to entertaining, with or without a spouse. As a result of opening my home, I received various invitations in return, not from the people who were my guests, but surprisingly from many other party givers. I learned to simplify my life.

CHAPTER 14

"Simplify, Simplify"

Simplify, simplify, intoned the actor quoting from Henry David Thoreau's *Walden, Life in the Woods* as hundreds of celebrants were stranded on Ellis Island, shivering in the windy rain, waiting to return to the mainland. It was July 4, 1986. America celebrated the 100th Anniversary of the Statue of Liberty with speeches, music, and fireworks. Millions, including me, watched this anniversary celebration on television while the participants found themselves in this collision of the best celebration with the worst weather in July. It typified the decade of the eighties—an era of excesses and extremes. No wonder the speechmaker chose to stress the nineteenth century philosophy of simplicity. It was such a paradox to call for simplicity in the midst of this twentieth-century traffic jam.

The decade of the eighties ushered in epidemics, terrorism, and natural and man-made disasters. Famine raged through Ethiopia. Earthquakes rocked Mexico City, remote Soviet Armenia, and nearby San Francisco, killing thousands of people. Disaster struck the NASA shuttle program when a faulty O-ring caused the Challenger to blow up, killing all aboard. A Soviet reactor at Chernobyl exploded, showering Europe with toxic fallout. The AIDS epidemic spread from adults to babies, and even the unborn were not spared.

But in the midst of tragedy, there were glimpses of hope, love, and joy. Millions prayed for Baby Jessica as rescuers tunneled down to save the infant trapped in a Texas well. We celebrated, via satellite, the royal wedding of Britain's Prince Andrew and Sarah Ferguson. And when the symbol of the Cold War, "die Mauer," opened up between East and West Germany, the jubilation and celebration among the people resembled "Christmas, New Year's, and Easter rolled into one," according to a West German radio announcer. These national and global events affected our lives in one way or another. None of them can be called "simple."

Simplicity can be defined as the opposite of excessiveness, something that is basic instead of extreme. One visible return to simple values can be witnessed in the enormous success of Robert Fulghum's book, *All I Really Need to Know I Learned in Kindergarten.* What he learned there were basic rules by which mankind lives and dies. President George Bush also called for a kinder, gentler nation.

But how do we *become* gentler, kinder, loving, more caring, when we find ourselves in traffic jams or are confronted with mounting monthly bills, growing frustrations, and demanding deadlines? We cannot return to the "good old days" or even "back to the future" as movies pretend.

We have to start with where we *are.* One phrase comes to mind: "Each day has enough trouble of its own" (Matthew 6:34 KJV). Jesus said it more than two thousand years ago. All the Thoreaus and Fulghums and speechwriters have borrowed from his teachings, adapting to suit their needs. "Come to Me, all who are weary and heavy laden, and I will give you rest," Jesus continues. "Take my yoke upon you and learn of me, for I am gentle and humble in heart; and you shall find rest for your souls." Jesus gives an invitation to come to Him with our burdens, frustrations, anger, disappointments, and anxieties.

Thoreau retreated to Walden to reflect upon life, exclaiming, "Simplify, simplify . . . let your affairs be as two or three and not a hundred or a thousand . . ." But Jesus, the Son of God, promises peace and rest in the midst of chaos and tragedy, so that we can go on with our lives. Yes, reflection is part of Jesus' teaching, too. "Consider the lilies how they grow, they neither toil nor spin—yet even Solomon in all his glory was not arrayed like one of these" (Matthew 6:28, 29 KJV). Jesus' teachings are simple and straightforward: "Ask and you will receive, seek and you will find; knock and the door will be opened."

CHAPTER 15

Marriage

It was during the nineties that another door opened for me. I met Robert Blum, a trust tax accountant and long distance runner. He invited me to run with him on the first of January 1993, destination, unknown to me. Well, after running through some snowy west side streets, we finally arrived at a church, located on the corner of Erin Avenue and West 32nd Street. The sign in front indicated that this was a Hispanic church.

"My grandfather was minister of this church in the thirties," Bob said.

"You're kidding!" I exclaimed. "What kind of church was it?"

"It was called Erin Avenue Baptist Church," he replied.

Now I was speechless. Erin Avenue Baptist Church was the mother-church of the church to which I belonged. I had often heard about Erin Avenue Baptist Church and how this German congregation looked for a new location to reach the post-war generation of young families. The new location turned out to be Parma Heights where a cornerstone was laid in 1954 for a new sanctuary, and where I worshipped when I met Bob.

Robert Blum loved to organize parties for the West Side Road Runners. I was an experienced hostess. So one month I invited the runners to my home to assemble the monthly newsletter. Bob was in charge. He saw to it that everyone had a task to perform: collating, folding, affixing address labels and stamps to each publication. I met a lot of new people and enjoyed the camaraderie of the running crowd.

One spring day in 1994 Bob asked me to marry him. It was a year-long engagement as we got to know each other and met each other's families and made new friends.

In 1995 we were invited to a Fourth of July celebration at my college friend Sandy's home.

As we were watching the fireworks in her front yard, Reverend Ralph Fotia asked me:

"Well, Christa, when are you and Bob getting married?"

"We have picked a date, but have not found a church yet," I replied.

"Well, I'll marry you at Epworth-Euclid," Reverend Fotia said.

Wow! What a great offer. Amidst fireworks and crackers going off, we made plans for our August 17th wedding, only six weeks away. Our theme song and verse was: "This is the day that the Lord has made, Let us rejoice and be glad in it."

And so it was, that Reverend Fotia married us in Epworth-Euclid Methodist Church at University Circle with family and friends in attendance. A dinner reception followed in the great hall downstairs. Jim Blum, Bob's brother, was the master of ceremonies, introducing our friends, who treated us to a musical medley. It was absolutely delightful. At the end, Bob sang to me "Love is a Many-Splendored Thing."

Wedding of Christa Eckert and Robert Blum. Christa's daughter Lynn and Robert's son Troy, witnesses.

CHAPTER 16

The Year 2000

When the United Methodist General Conference 2000, was held in Cleveland, my husband Bob and I led several walking tours of downtown for many of the foreign delegates and visitors. Estonians that we had met the year before were among them, too.

On one of the walks past city hall the group stopped to admire the free stamp sculpture by Claes Oldenburg. It is a huge, dark red, rubber-stamp sculpture lying on its side with the letters E E R F printed backwards (as are all letters on a rubber stamp). The visitors from Eastern Europe were puzzled by the meaning of this sculpture. When Bob explained that the letters spelled out

"FREE," the related word being *freedom*, their faces lit up in recognition. For many of them, the freedom to worship and to attend the General Conference had only recently become a reality after the fall of Communism.

In Christ we are free indeed, even when there is threat of persecution and oppression, because of our Christian faith. Our freedom in Christ is not a "free" rubber stamp to do whatever we want, but to reflect His teachings in our life.

Christ's teachings had a great impact on my own academic career at Case Western Reserve University where I taught German from 1987–2000. After the General Conference ended in May 2000, I had an appointment at CWRU. I parked my car at University Circle and walked along the fairly deserted college campus, reflecting on my teaching days and how many lives I had touched instructing all levels of German to undergrads and graduate students. On my walk I picked up a dollar bill on the sidewalk of Bellflower Road, just where Freiberger Library used to be. The building was gone and a grassy field spanned the space from Bellflower to the new Kelvin Smith Library, built in 1997 in classical architectural style. The bust of Harold Hart Crane (1899–1932) still stood on the steps leading to the former Freiberger Library. It was erected by sculptor William McVey in 1985 the year Richard died. Next to the pedestal, facing south toward the new library, was this inscription on a bronze tablet, a poem by Hart Crane:

> The image word, it is, that holds
> Hushed willows anchored in its glow.
> It is the unbetrayable reply
> Whose accent no farewell can know.[1]

"No farewell" is what came to my mind, too, as I walked past the familiar campus with Guilford House in the background, yellow and bright, the house in which I spent thirteen years, emerging to the waiting students in the classroom, eager to learn German.

It was time to go. It was not as exciting now as it was in the beginning of the summer of August 1987 when I was hired by Professor Strauss to teach German. At that time, I was still grieving and coming to terms with my widowhood. All at once, I had a job, and students looked up to me and respected me and listened to what I had to say.

So today, upon retirement, when I had to choose between roll-over, cash-out or annuity, I chose annuity. I found out that means that for the rest of my life, CWRU's bursar deposits an amount into my checking account. It is a fair sum. It gives me the benefits I am entitled to after thirteen years of employment at the University.

I wanted to cry as I walked along Bellflower, but I did not. I felt "unbetrayable" like Crane Hart, the poet, or like Bernhard Schlink, the author of *Der Vorleser*. I paid my $2.00 parking, and when the clerk asked, "Do you like a receipt?" I replied: "Yes." It was after I had found the $1.00 bill on the sidewalk. So I really paid only $1.00. The sidewalk symbolically rewarded me for all the steps I had taken between Guilford House and Freiberger Library.

"The hushed Willows" were glowing and glad that I had made that return trip to campus. I drove in my car past the Museum, down to Martin Luther King, Jr. Drive where the road winds alongside the Nationality Gardens, past the Hungarian site, the Estonian Flagpole with its black, blue, and white flag, past the Goethe-and-Schiller monument. I always had told my students of German that this monument was the identical one erected in Weimar, Germany, and there is another identical one in Milwaukee, Wisconsin.

As I approached the end of the MLK, Jr. parkway, I swung to the right and entered the

Shoreway leading west along Lake Erie. "Die Schwalbe fliegt über'n Eriesee" (Over Lake Erie the "Swallow" takes flight), the John Maynard Poem came to mind. Tante Ursula quoted to me the poem she had learned as a child in Berlin when she finally got to see "Eriesee" on her visit in 2000 to Cleveland from her native Germany. It was her first trip to America after her husband's death, my father's younger brother. She came with her son, my cousin Alexander. What a grand time we had that summer. We talked about family and relatives and reminders of the past.

One reminder is a wooden box, which sits on my desk. It has carvings all around the lid and on all four sides. On the side facing me there is a smiling sunrise with rays radiating to the lid. When I open the box, I see it's lined in red velvet. It's a jewelry box, which belonged to my mother. After she died, I took the box. No expensive valuables are in the box. There's a carved ivory bead necklace, a golden circle pin with a pink stone in the center, and another gold pin with straight solid gold double bars that is decorated with pearls and precious stones. It is a very old piece, which my mother had ever since I could remember. There are other gold pins, shaped like circles and bows and flowers in the box. She used to fasten her scarves with these pins. The two-bar gold pin came from Latvia. She had it with her when we fled the advancing Russian troops.

My mother, known as Oma to her grandchildren, loved to serve ginger ale with every meal. She did not drink beer, but sometimes a glass of wine. When we went out to eat, she usually ordered ginger ale to go along with her meal and sipped it through a straw. She had a delightful European accent. It was hard to detect where she came from. Was it German, was it Swedish, was it Estonian?

When Oma last ordered a ginger ale, I remember the waitress coming around again and asking, "Will there be anything else?"

"Yes," my mother answered with her German accent, "a Stroh." Was she ever amazed when the waitress came back with a beer, a Stroh's beer. She wanted a *straw,* which in German is pronounced "stroh" the word for straw. We had a good laugh about this mispronunciation. May she rest in peace.

---

[1]Hart Crane *Voyages VI* 1920 (Oldpoetry.com) Public Domain

CHAPTER 17

Close to Home

This week I stayed close to home even though I was supposed to fly to Washington, DC for a conference for foreign language teachers (ACTFL). When I heard about the plane crash on Tuesday in New York (Queens), that was it. I talked to my daughter Lynn the day before about maybe not going and she said:

"Well, if you don't want to fly, don't go!"

So the next day I cancelled my flight, my hotel reservations and wrote a letter to retrieve my conference registration fee. I felt good.

The next day, I had lunch with my brother Kuno at Yours Truly on Shaker Square. He told me about his trip to Paris last month with Nijole, his wife. They loved staying in Montmartre, visiting the artists' galleries and little shops. I could picture myself there.

After lunch I drove to my son Tom's place in Shaker Heights, and sure enough he was there. Jim, his landlord, opened the door and was delighted to see me. I told him I was sorry we missed Patty's Party, but we'll come next time.

"Don't wait that long," he said.

Patty is Jim's black spaniel dog and Patty's Party is always on August 2, which actually is Jim's birthday. The whole Parkland neighborhood is invited to this backyard birthday bash with lots of food and drinks, a cake, and live music. As Jim and I were talking, Tom came ambling out of his room.

I said, "I'll give you a ride to Lakewood, and you can finish up installing the Adobe Acrobat Reader."

"O.K.," he said and off we went.

Tom is so knowledgeable with computers. But then when he was working on my computer, down-loading the Adobe File, he said: "Mom, your computer does not have enough memory for this file. You need a new computer!"

Well, thanks. We'll just leave it without the Adobe file. Then my daughter Lynn and my granddaughter Ariana stopped by my place while Tom was here and we had tea together.

It was heart-warming to be with my adult children close to home this week. I could go on . . . My colleague Virginia Jones invited me to see the Musical *Annie* at the Near West Theatre. And we went. I picked her up, and we had dinner at a place nearby. There are lots of children in the play, acting as orphans in a nineteenth-century orphanage where *Annie* is trying to escape. I had never seen the play. Many familiar tunes in this play lead me to hum along: "Tomorrow, tomorrow . . . you're always a day away."

The music in me lingers on. I wonder, what is my instrument?

I have heard that the writer's voice corresponds to a musical instrument. Off the top of my head, I thought I was a flute. Karin, my daughter, plays the flute, and I always admired her for this talent of making people happy with her music. However, I feel that I am a cello. This instrument has a wonderful mellow sound, and in a string quartet you cannot do without a cello. It gives the supporting tenor voice, which blends with the other three string instruments. A cello is also superb when heard in solo performance. It has a rich warm sound. I attended a concert where two cello players performed together. It lifted my spirits. The music was warm, exciting, also spirited and soul-searching. I hope I project some of these qualities as a writer.

When I was in high school, I was assigned to play the cello in the concert orchestra. I enjoyed being the only cello player, and I had an important role. The string bass player, also the only one, and we developed a close friendship because of our unique roles. I never pursued the cello after high school. I had no cello of my own, so I continued playing the piano. It was much later in life, as an adult, married with children, that my mother told me that Samuelson's, our Swedish-American church sponsors, offered to sell me their own cello when I was in high school. But my parents didn't buy it because they couldn't afford it. I felt sad, when I heard that. Maybe I would have become a great cello player.

CHAPTER 18

Ground Zero

Ground Zero, New York City

It was the Memorial Day weekend 2002 when Bob and I arrived in New York City. Last year's 9/11 attack on the World Trade Center where over 3,000 people lost their lives is still on people's mind. However, with another threat of terrorism hanging over the city, the people seemed calm, even playful.

"We cannot stay inside for fear," said one woman at the Brooklyn Deli where I had bought cold cuts and bread for lunch.

"That's what they want—for us to be afraid and stay inside."

New Yorkers were out on the street, walking, talking, shopping, and hailing taxis. At a nearby playground where we went with three-year-old Janine, our granddaughter, we heard many foreign languages spoken by young mothers and their children: Russian, Arabic, and Chinese. There were happy children's sounds coming from the squeaky swings, "wheee" sounds from the slides and jungle gyms. It was the international language of children at play, all at once interrupted by Janine's musical sneakers jingling, "It's a small world after all, it's a small, small world." Janine giggled and didn't want the music to stop. No terrorism here on the playground.

She was looking forward to the Memorial Day Parade and seeing the mounted police. And indeed, the parade proceeded as scheduled on Monday morning at ten o'clock. People of all ages and nationalities lined Fourth Avenue in Brooklyn. Soon we heard the marching music played by the Fort Hamilton High School Band leading the parade. Politicians, city officials and Miss Norway (many Norwegians settled in Brooklyn in the nineteenth century) sat in open cars and waved to the crowd. War veterans handed out American flags to children on the sidewalk. Members of all four branches of the military marched along the parade route, the army, the navy, the airforce, and the marines. The biggest cheer and applause swelled up when the fire engines passed by with our heroes waving and returning the smiles. Children scrambled for hard candy tossed to them.

The next day Bob and I had to go to Ground Zero, site of the 9/11 destruction, to see for ourselves what makes New Yorkers survive. We took the R-train to Whitehall Station in Manhattan, walked past the bookstores, flower stands, and outdoor cafés to South Street Seaport. Here we asked for a free ticket to Ground Zero. We walked up toward St. Paul's Chapel of Trinity Church. We entered the boardwalk constructed along the wrought iron cemetery fence of St. Paul's Chapel. All the names of the fallen heroes were inscribed on a huge computer-generated poster, almost as long as the Vietnam Wall in Washington DC. We walked slowly, reading just a few of the names:

John Patrick Hart
Michelle Henrique
Martin Garner
Victoria Alvarez-Brito
Steve Mercado

We don't know any of these people who had died. But our hearts ached, and we cried quietly.

The people around us stood in silence on the platform overlooking the crater that was once the World Trade Center. We walked down the wooden exit ramp. Along that wall, fresh carnations have been placed in glass vials, next to posters, flags and ribbons with photos and names of the victims. Messages were handwritten on the wooden space framing the memorials. So we wrote a message, too: "And God shall wipe away every tear from their eyes; and there shall no longer be any death; there shall no longer be any mourning, or crying, or pain;" (Revelation 21:4 NASV).

Many nationalities were represented among those who perished in the World Trade Center. America is a land of immigrants and this writer has made the immigrant's journey to experience the joys, the pains, the triumphs and defeats, the wonder of childbirth and the mystery of death, only a heartbeat away. As a Christian, I claim the promise of life after death, in that Christ has conquered death in his Resurrection. So when we experience the "not-again" cry, we know that in the end there will be no more crying or pain. But in the meantime we continue to journey on this planet and write about it for those who come after us.

"Not Again" stated the cover on *Newsweek* and "Tears and Tributes for Columbia Crew" read the headline of the February 5, 2003, *Plain Dealer*. Reading about the seven astronauts who perished in the Columbia shuttle, we were convinced that they truly believed in their mission and knew the risk involved. This was an international crew, and the whole world was grieving.

Throughout generations people have stood up and died for what they believed in. Leo Tolstoy claimed that the secret of life is not in staying alive but in finding something to live for.

In Europe, March 8th was first officially recognized as International Women's Day in 1911. More than sixty-seven years later an Education Task Force in California selected March eighth to celebrate Women's History Week. Three years later the United States Congress passed a resolution establishing National Women's History Week, co-sponsored by Senator Orrin Hatch and Representative Barbara Mikulski. Another proclamation in 1987 expanded the week to a month in celebration of women's contributions to history. Schools began to host Women's History Week programs, reading about Mary Todd Lincoln, Harriet Tubman, Eleanor Roosevelt, and many others. Colleges and universities established women studies curriculums.

So it is fitting that we honor and remember the two women who were part of the Columbia crew, Laurel Clark and Kalpana Chawla, both forty-one. Both women were married. Dr. Clark was born in Iowa and leaves behind a husband and an eight-year-old son Iain. She loved many things, nature, hiking, camping, and scuba diving. She wanted to become a pediatrician. She came from such a large family, that seemed out of reach, but she pursued her dream and earned her MD from the University of Wisconsin. She applied to NASA to begin training as a flight surgeon and was accepted after an initial rejection. When school children asked her for advice she said: "Do what it is you love to do. You'll do a really good job at it because you love it."[2] She echoes what the Apostle Paul writes to the Colossians: "Whatsoever you do, do your work heartily, as for the Lord, rather than for men" (Col. 3:23 NASV). Clark really felt blessed to view Earth from space. "It is spectacular," she wrote in an e-mail shortly before she died.

Kalpana Chawla also had a passion for space travel. Looking out the window of the shuttle she wrote, "The Nile River looks like a lifeline in the Sahara . . . Earth is very beautiful. I wish everyone could see it." Chawla was born in Karnal, India, and emmigrated to the United States in the 1980s. She dreamed of one day owning a telescope and gazing at the stars. Her first trip into space was in 1997. After earning her PhD in aerospace engineering, she was hired by NASA as an astronaut trainee. She had close ties with the children of the school in India where she attended as a youngster. She told the students to follow their dream, which is what she did. Even if we who remain are not called upon to die for what we believe in, we must not compromise our Christian faith but remain faithful and true.

[2]*Newsweek*, February 10, 2003.

CHAPTER 19

Highlights

Bob and I never send out Christmas letters, but here is one that I almost sent out because it summarizes some of the highpoints of 2003.

Christmas 2003
Christa Eckert Blum and Bob Blum

"Set up for yourself roadmarks,
Place for yourself guideposts,
Direct your mind to the highway,
The way by which you went."
Jeremiah 31:21 NASV

The highway by which Bob and I went this last year led us to New York City and later to Scotland, to the Loch Ness at Inverness, where we did not see the Loch Ness Monster. But we heard some incredible stories form our tour guide about St. Columba, the Irish priest, who brought Christianity to Scotland in the sixth century. We heard about Columba's sighting of the Loch Ness Monster as recorded in his diary. As he and his brave band of men arrived at the Loch or lake, Columba said to his men: "I'll swim across the lake." None of his men wanted to swim with him. So he said to them: "I'll meet you on the other shore." Leaving his robe on the stony beach he waded into the shallow waters and began to swim toward the center of the lake. With the distant shore in sight, he perceived a monstrous snakelike creature surfacing from the frigid glacial lake. Columba looked up and saw the red eyes of this creature, saw the mouth opened and rows of very sharp teeth, so sharp, the light glinted off the tips of each one. Columba's next move was to pray, asking for deliverance from the monster if it were God's will. The tour guide tells this version of Columba's deliverance. "Well, God came down and whispered into the monster's ear: 'Monster, I'm so disappointed in you. You are about to eat and kill my messenger, St. Columba. He is about to go all over Scotland, spreading my Word, the Love of Jesus Christ to the people.' The monster drew back and cried out:

'I was going to eat St. Columba! I am so ashamed of myself.' The monster dove down to the bottom of the Loch and hardly ever shows himself at all. Except on cloudy, overcast days, on rare occasions, one might see the monster appear on the surface of the Loch." To this day St. Columba, who died at age seventy-six at Iona, is hailed as the first Christian missionary to Scotland.

Our reason for being in Scotland was to attend the wedding of Bob's son Jay to Helen, his Scottish bride from Perth. (I sat next to Sir Walter Scott's Fair Maid of Perth, cast in stone on a bench). The wedding ceremony was held in an old stone church where Helen's parents had been married and where the priest had baptized Helen. The same priest also performed the wedding ceremony for Helen and Jay. It was a traditional Scottish wedding with the groom and groom's men wearing the tartan kilts, and a bagpiper announcing the arrival of the bridal party. This wedding was the first of three we attended this summer.

In July we witnessed the solemn vows taken by Brenda and Bob aboard the Nautica Queen in the Flats in Cleveland. Family and friends, we were in the friends category, gathered aboard the ship for a cruise in the harbor while being served a fine dinner, watching the sunset on Lake Erie, later dancing on deck and doing the conga line from upper deck to lower deck. It kept my heart pounding in perfect rhythm. Oh, I forgot to tell you that the first guidepost along our 2003 journey was open-heart surgery for me on January 6th, an epiphany I will never forget. My daughter Lynn, my granddaughter Ariana, and I were on our way to Cancun to spend the end of the year on a warm beach. Aboard the airliner, I passed out and Lynn, my physician daughter, shook me: "Mom wake up, wake up." I didn't want to wake up. But she insisted and alerted the flight attendants and the pilot to land the plane. Only ten minutes into our flight, Columbus was the next available airport. So after the plane landed, I wobbled down the aisle of the plane, with passengers staring at me, finally reaching the stretcher waiting for me outside the plane. An ambulance transported me to the hospital in Columbus and later back to Cleveland. I felt bad for my eight-year-old granddaughter having to miss the warm beach scene because of Nana. But Ariana was more concerned about my well being than playing on a tropical beach.

Bob cared for me during my post-surgery recovery. He did the laundry, cleaned the house, prepared meals, dressed me, and cared for me in a way only a loving husband can. He enjoyed caring for me so much that later this year he enrolled in a training course to become a nurse's assistant. After having retired from Key Corps as a trust tax accountant, he was looking for some part-time employment. He didn't have to wait long to find employment. Several nursing homes wanted to hire him.

The third wedding we attended was my daughter Lynn's in August. She married Tom Tomasula in an outdoor wedding at Glidden House. About one hundred guests gathered under the summer sun to witness the solemn ceremony, which also included eight-year-old Ariana as Tom adopted her as his daughter. Bob and I also hosted the wedding rehearsal and dinner right here in our great garden overlooking the Metro Park.

In the middle of July, Bob and I and some of our Scenic Park neighbors hosted the first ever "blighted block party" to which all of Lakewood was invited. It was a great success with a strolling barbershop quartet, music by the praise team from Rocky River United Methodist Church, lots of hot dogs, hamburgers and cotton candy free of charge, games for the kids, and a walking tour of the neighborhood led by yours truly. As some of you know, our homes in Scenic Park have been declared blighted so that they can be taken by eminent domain to make room for upscale condominiums, offices, shops, and a ten-screen movie theater overlooking the Metro Park. Of course we fought with all our might against this eminent domain abuse. After Mike Wallace, of 60 Minutes fame, aired a program about "Bogus Blight," interviewing our neighbor the Saleets and Mayor Madeline Cain of Lakewood, the issue of abuse became of national concern, and people started calling and e-mailing the Saleets to show support for keeping their home.

Well, to make a long story short, a referendum was put on the November 4 election ballot, which would decide the fate of the West End Project, known as Issue 47. We won by forty-seven votes, even after a recount of each ballot by hand. Not only did we receive national coverage to our plight, but international attention as well. My cousin Boris, who lives in

Belgium, visited in July. He was outraged at the monstrosity of labeling our neighborhood blighted. "You have not seen blight," he announced while breakfasting at our umbrella table surrounded by luscious foliage, chirping birds and begging squirrels. We celebrated the Fourth of July on Public Square to the strains of the Cleveland Orchestra. He had never heard the orchestra live, and we were lucky to get seats in the VIP section because of Boris's diplomatic connections.

Another visitor from Germany was from my nephew Hans-Hagen who visited us at the end of October just before the November 4 election. As an attorney, he was keenly interested in this issue to see American politics at work.

We are blessed to have freedom of speech, freedom to own property, freedom to worship and pray. At this Christmas we thank God for our many blessings we received along the way. "Our God is an awesome God."

MERRY CHRISTMAS!

EPILOGUE

A Treasure in My Heart

February is heart month. Everywhere there are red hearts decorating store windows and walls. People are encouraged to send cards to their sweethearts on Valentine's Day. The human heart is designated as the seat of emotions, of passions, of spirituality, and of course, as the physical life-giving mechanism. When the heart stops beating, physical life ends.

In the Bible there are so many references to the heart. Here are just a few that come to mind:

Love the Lord with all your heart
Let not your heart be troubled

Making melody with your heart
Intentions of the heart
Joyful heart
broken and contrite heart
sincere heart
a clean heart

So the heart runs the whole range of emotions. The saying "All head and no heart" means that a person only uses his mind and not his heart in making decisions. My heart and my mind were both out of commission when I underwent heart surgery on January 6th. Before the coronary bypass graft, the surgeon explained to me the procedure and said that I had to go into the surgery with a positive attitude. I wanted to know my options. There were no options. I could forego surgery, but sooner or later the blocked artery would lead to a heart attack or stroke or death. So I put myself into the hands of the capable surgeon who asked me, just before I was wheeled into surgery, whether people were praying for me and who was out there in the waiting room. I almost choked up when I realized that my family was "out there" praying for me. I said: "Yes." So with the prayer support of my family and friends and church members, I came through surgery successfully.

Thank you everyone who prayed for me. God answers prayer. I am recovering nicely with Bob at my side. Thank you for the many encouraging cards, notes, e-mails, visits, and flowers I received. I am overwhelmed by the love and passion pouring out from your hearts. I treasure all these things in my heart and mind, just like "Mary treasured up all these things, pondering them in her heart" (Luke 2:19 NASV).

To order additional copies of

In a Heartbeat

Have your credit card ready and call:

1-877-421-READ (7323)

or please visit our web site at
www.pleasantword.com

Also available at:
www.amazon.com
and
www.barnesandnoble.com

Printed in the United States
33643LVS00001B/97-144

9 781414 102528